AN AGGRESSION MANAGEMENT WORKBOOK

ANGER MANAGEMENT ESSENTIALS

TEEN EDITION

Anita Avedian
Licensed Marriage and Family Therapist
Certified Anger Management Specialist-IV

Ingrid Caswell
Licensed Marriage and Family Therapist
Certified Anger Management Specialist-III

ILLUSTRATED BY GARYL B. ARANETA

Acknowledgements

Many thanks to those who have contributed to the making of *Anger Management Essentials, Teen Edition*, especially the wonderful, ever-evolving Anger Management 818 team.

Our gratitude to...

Arati Patel, for her contribution to the section on bullying...

Gayane Aramyan, for tirelessly formatting and coordinating illustrations while simultaneously working towards Marriage and Family Therapist licensure...

Garyl B. Araneta, who turned our abstract concepts into images of living, breathing people...

Bill Weiner, for photographing and designing our cover with his signature passion and humor...

Bryce Caswell, for the use of his image and representation of the challenge that is adolescence...

Sylvia Cary, for her sage consultation along the road to book publishing...

and to the California Association of Anger Management Providers (CAAMP) and the National Association of Anger Management Providers (NAMA), who have taken the lead in providing, encouraging, and supporting standards and ethics in the field of anger management.

Table of Contents

Welcome to *Anger Management Essentials, Teen Edition*!

Since you're reading this, you're probably struggling with anger. Maybe your anger has cost you a lot: freedom, self-esteem, relationships, opportunities. Maybe you're feeling beaten-down and doubtful about whether there is anything you can do to improve the way you handle anger. Many teens approach this workbook with resistance because they fear it might be a waste of time. Later, those same teens express surprise and gratitude that these exercises have changed their behavior and, as a result, they are getting what they want. The tools and skills you will learn here will serve you not only throughout your teen years but the rest of your life. They will guide you in forming strong, satisfying, lifelong relationships. More importantly, they will help you manage relationships that are difficult and less rewarding. No matter how others behave, these skills will help you walk through life as the person you want to be.

What to Expect

To get the most out of this anger management workbook, you must practice the skills between groups/sessions. Coming to the class, paying attention and even sharing with your group is not enough to make real behavioral change. The skills taught in each lesson must be practiced throughout the week, every time you find yourself in an upsetting situation. You then come back into the next group/session and talk about how you used the tool and what the result was. Your group facilitator will coach you through the best use of these skills by asking questions such as, "How did you do?" and "How could you have done better?" Just like with raising your grades, it's not enough to *know* that you need to do homework and study for tests; you have to actually *do* it!

How to Do It

1. Commit to making a change. Complete the lessons in this workbook and practice them daily.

2. Be open. Be aware of your own thoughts and feelings, notice physical signs of anger in your body, and accept feedback from others.

3. Be proactive. Plan ahead to avoid anger-triggering situations.

Checking In

If you are using this workbook in a group that does check-ins, follow the format below. (This will also be the structure that you use to express yourself in most of the exercises in this book and in your future, real-life communication with others.)

1. Tell what happened (the upsetting situation) in a few (three or four) sentences.

> *Example: My parents told me that I have to turn my phone in at 10 PM on school nights.*

2. What thought did you have about the situation? (What did you tell yourself was happening?)

> *Example: They want to be mean and controlling for no reason.*

3. How did you feel?

> *Example: Frustrated and hopeless.*

4. What did you do (action)?

> *Example: I refused to bring my phone to them at 10 and got into a physical tug-of-war over it with my Dad. It fell on the floor and shattered.*

5. What would you like from the group now? To simply listen? Or to give you feedback?

> *Example: I'd like to know what you guys think I could have done differently.*

What Do You Know About Anger?

What is anger?

Anger is a **feeling** – a powerful and perfectly normal human emotion. Don't confuse it with aggression. Aggression is a *behavior*.

Anger is a **signal** that something is not OK with us and we need to change it. Anger needs to be expressed in order for us to get what we need, but there are helpful and unhelpful ways of expressing it.

Finally, anger is **energy** – it gives us confidence and motivation to take action and make positive changes in our lives.

Let's look at healthy anger in action: if a friend arrives half an hour late to meet you at the mall and you feel upset, your anger is a signal that being on time is important to you. Anger gives you the confidence to ask your friend to let you know in advance if she's going to be late.

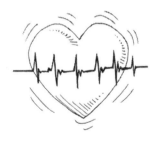

What happens to your body when you're angry?

Some possibilities are: dry mouth, rapid heart beat, hot skin, upset stomach, clenched jaw, stiff neck, grinding teeth, tunnel vision, and muscle tension.

Why does this happen?

When we think we're being threatened in some way, the oldest part of our brain, the amygdala, sends a message to our body to get ready to fight or run.

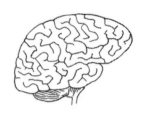

This is known as our 'fight or flight' response. It makes our heart beat faster, our muscles tense up, etc. It prepares the body to *react* before we can *think*. The newest part of our brain, the prefrontal cortex, is our 'brake system'. It's the part of our brain that says, "Wait, if you do this, what might happen? Will you regret it?" The prefrontal cortex calms us down and gives us time to make responsible choices.

In caveman times, the people who survived were the ones with the strongest amygdalae – those who could fight or run away from danger. But in today's modern age, we no longer face the kinds of threats the cavemen faced. The problem is that our bodies haven't changed. For survival, we are naturally wired to *react* before we *think* about the consequences of our actions. We're built to fight or run, even when the situation that we're facing isn't life-threatening. That's why we get so upset when someone cuts in front of us in line, although we're not actually in any danger.

The purpose of the anger management exercises in this book is to train your prefrontal cortex - your brake system - to kick into gear immediately after your amygdala is triggered to fight or run. This way you can avoid doing something that is damaging to yourself or others. The more you practice using your anger management tools, the more control you will have over your anger.

CALL TO ACTION: This week, talk to someone about something you learned from this worksheet. ("Did you know....?) When you teach someone something you've just learned, you strengthen your own knowledge.

Working on My Anger...What's in It for Me?

Have you ever had a goal to change something about yourself but had no interest in doing the necessary work? Maybe you wanted to lose weight, but you weren't ready to cut calories. Maybe you wanted better grades, but you weren't willing to spend less time playing video games in order to study.

When we're struggling with motivation, it can be very helpful to identify the reasons we want to make changes. Ask yourself, "How would I be different if I made this change?" or "What would be different in my life?" Before starting this program, let's assess your level of motivation and reasons for wanting to change. It will help you feel more open to the information in this workbook.

To start, list below your reasons for wanting to change. When it comes to anger, people usually want to change because of a painful incident that got them into trouble. What are your reasons for wanting to work on your anger now? How would life be different if you were calmer?

1. _____
2. _____
3. _____

On a scale of 1-10, 10 being very motivated and 1 being completely unmotivated, how would you rate your level of motivation to work on your anger? Circle one.

1   2   3   4   5   6   7   8   9   10

On a scale of 1-10, 10 being your most willing and 1 being completely unwilling, how willing are you to change your reactions when you get upset?

(Hint: This question is asking how likely you are to do the work needed to change.)

1   2   3   4   5   6   7   8   9   10

Working on your anger is an ongoing process. Remember that a great strategy to help you stay motivated is to remind yourself of all the reasons why you want to be calm, grounded and in control of yourself.
Some common reasons that people want to work on their anger include:

1. My anger scares students at my school, and I don't want to scare people.

2. I get feedback from teachers on my report cards that my behavior is poor. It's time to make a change.

3. I could get accepted to the college of my choice if I just put effort into managing my stress and being more relaxed.

4. When I learn to express myself in a calmer way, I'll get better responses from people.

Make a list of advantages to being calmer and more understanding in the section below:

1. _____
2. _____
3. _____

Add to this list when you think of additional advantages. It helps to have this in your notes app on your phone so that the list is available to read whenever you're struggling with motivation.

> **CALL TO ACTION:** Read your list of **Advantages to Working on My Anger** daily for the next month. It will help you shift your focus and get into a more positive mindset. On the days you read this list, you may have a better attitude towards those around you - and life in general.

Anger as a Mask

Though we may not realize it, we feel vulnerable emotions, like fear and sadness, in the moment just before we experience anger. These vulnerable feelings are called "primary emotions", and they can be very hard to tolerate. Anger often comes up as a cover for anxiety, hurt, helplessness, embarrassment, and humiliation. We skip right over feeling our primary emotions and go right to anger because it helps us to feel less vulnerable.

Here's an example: Let's say that someone cuts in front of you in the lunch line. You may feel humiliated or "threatened" (taken advantage of in front of others). Humiliation will come up first. Then anger will come up second to cover the pain of the humiliation. Humiliation is the natural, first-level emotion in response to feeling threatened. Anger is the secondary, protective response.

What About You?

1. Recall a past incident when you felt angry. Summarize it in two or three sentences.

_____

_____

_____

2. What upset you about the situation?

_____

3. Is it possible you felt anything before anger? Hurt, embarrassment, fear, etc.? What emotion was your anger mask hiding?

_____

Now What?

Now that I know what painful emotion my anger is covering, what do I do with that feeling? People hear us better when we communicate our vulnerable emotions. Your next step is to communicate your vulnerable feelings to someone involved in an upsetting incident. (This is not safe to do with everyone. You'll need to decide who are the people in your life that can handle sensitive issues, and who are those that can't.)

CALL TO ACTION: The next time you get upset, pay attention to the feeling that your anger is hiding. If you've determined this is a safe person to share with, communicate this emotion to that person. (Communication skills will be covered in a separate lesson.)

Keeping Track of My Anger

Have you ever noticed that the way you handle a situation doesn't get you what you want? Sometimes it will be impossible to get certain things from certain people because they just don't have it to give. But there are other times when our own behavior is what is keeping us from getting what we want. The good news is that if we're the cause of the problem, we can also be the solution. Tracking your angry episodes after they've happened puts events into perspective so that you can make different choices in the future. Let's look at how to track angry episodes.

Situation 1:

1. What happened? *I didn't get invited to a party.*

2. What did you want to happen? *I wanted to be invited.*

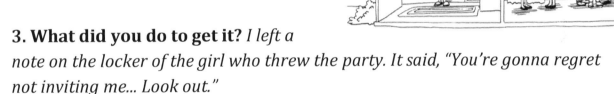

3. What did you do to get it? *I left a note on the locker of the girl who threw the party. It said, "You're gonna regret not inviting me... Look out."*

4. Did you get what you wanted? Yes <u>No</u> Somewhat

5. What happened after you did that (#3)? *The person found out that I left the note on her locker and reported it to the principal. I was expelled from school.*

6. Did anyone get hurt physically? Yes <u>No</u> **Emotionally?** <u>Yes</u> No
If yes, how? *The person probably felt scared and threatened when she got the note. I felt humiliated because everyone in school found out about the note and my expulsion.*

7. What could you have done differently to get what you wanted (#2)? *I could have just asked if I could come to the party. Or I could have planned my own fun night with people I like to be with.*

<u>**Situation 2:**</u>

1. What happened? *My girlfriend was talking to a guy at school.*

2. What did you want to happen? *I wanted to feel important to her.*

3. What did you do to get it? *I told her she can't talk to other guys.*

4. Did you get what you wanted?
Yes <u>No</u> Somewhat

5. What happened after you did that (#3)? *She told me I'm ridiculous and broke up with me.*

6. Did anyone get hurt physically? Yes <u>No</u> **Emotionally?** <u>Yes</u> No **If yes, how?** *I'm so upset because I didn't want to break up with her. I miss her and I really regret what I did.*

7. What could you have done differently to get what you wanted (#2)? *I could have talked to her about my feelings and told her what I would need to feel important in the relationship. I could have talked about it with a friend and gotten their take on the situation. I could have looked at the real reasons I was feeling insecure and worked on my own self-esteem.*

> **CALL TO ACTION:** Complete the following anger log every time you have an angry episode. You can make as many copies of the blank log as you need, or you can ask your counselor for copies.

Anger Log

Today's Date: _____   Date of Incident: _____

1. What happened?

_____

_____

_____

2. What did you want to happen? (This response should identify a vulnerable need. For example, the need to be heard, cared about, special, important).

_____

_____

3. What did you do to get it?

_____

_____

4. Did you get what you wanted?   Yes   No   Somewhat

5. What happened after you did that (#3)?

_____

_____

6. Did anyone get hurt physically? Yes   No
   Emotionally? Yes   No   If yes, how?

_____

_____

7. What could you have done differently to get what you wanted (#2)?

_____

_____

What Bugs You?
Anger-Triggering Situations and Pet Peeves

Ready to see what really triggers you? If a situation below does not bother you at all, write a 0 on the line next to it. If it bugs you a little, write a 1. If you get annoyed when it happens, write a 2. Write a 3 if it really frustrates you.

0-No trigger   1-Mild trigger   2-Moderate trigger   3-Severe trigger

General Situations
__ 1. When people show off, name drop or "perform" for others
__ 2. Petty theft, such as pens and pencils
__ 3. Someone cutting ahead of you in line
__ 4. People who won't take "No" for an answer
__ 5. Loud gum chewing and cracking
__ 6. People who talk too much
__ 7. People who lie
__ 8. People who gossip

Phone
__ 1. Phone screen breaks
__ 2. Someone tries to get your password
__ 3. Phone doesn't work properly
__ 4. Forget to charge your phone
__ 5. Friend borrows your charger and returns it damaged.

Social Media
__ 1. People who refuse to learn about new technology
__ 2. People who post lies about others on social media
__ 3. Someone posts or tags a picture of you without your consent
__ 4. Seeing pictures of your friends getting together without you
__ 5. Seeing on social media that your ex is in another relationship
__ 6. People who share too much about themselves for attention

__ 7. Catfishing (making fake profiles)

__ 8. Someone stalking you online

__ 9. Getting bullied online

__ 10. Someone video taping you and posting without your knowledge

__ 11. People constantly checking their social media

Financial

__ 1. Friends suggesting expensive restaurants you can't afford

__ 2. Losing a wallet, cell phone, credit card, etc.

__ 3. Not being able to afford to go on a trip that your friends will go on

__ 4. Being ripped off

__ 5. Not being ablc to afford clothes that everyone else is wearing

__ 6. Going out with friends who don't pay enough to cover the bill

__ 7. Getting a parking ticket when you're two minutes late to the meter

__ 8. Friends borrowing money and not paying it back

Relationships

__ 1. People who talk about others behind their backs

__ 2. People who flake

__ 3. People who don't keep their word

__ 4. A friend dating your ex

__ 5. People who have "hidden agendas"

__ 6. Partner cheating on you

__ 7. Partner talking to someone of the opposite gender

Family

__ 1. Strict parents

__ 2. Parents who don't 'get it'

__ 3. Parents who say "No" to everything

__ 4. Annoying siblings

__ 5. Family members with alcohol or other drug problems

__ 6. Family yelling and fighting

__ 7. Mom/Dad going through your journal

__ 8. Mom/Dad checking your social media accounts

__ 9. Family member not knocking before coming into your room

__ 10. Parent not being as involved with you as you'd like

Driving/ Car Related

__ 1. Tailgating

__ 2. Aggressive or show-off driving

__ 3. People who talk on the phone while driving, even where it's illegal to do so

__ 4. A driver texting at a red light who doesn't notice when the light turns green

__ 5. Women putting on makeup while driving

__ 6. People eating while driving

__ 7. Being a passenger in a car with a reckless driver

CALL TO ACTION: Now that you are more aware of the specific things that bother you, notice this week whether you have a little more patience with them. Simple awareness can go a long way toward reducing frustration.

Chill! Quick Tips to Cooling Down

We live in a fast-paced world. It seems like almost every day a new technology pops up to solve a problem. So it makes sense that when we're in emotional pain, we want it relieved immediately. Here are some quick tips to calm you down when you're starting to get vexed.

1. Walk Away - When things get heated, leave. Being around the trigger of your anger will only escalate it. Changing the scene interrupts the amygdala's hijacking of the brain and prevents you from making a situation worse. Walking away gives you time to think rationally about what your next move will be.

2. Count to Ten - Counting disrupts emotion. Emotion is managed in the right hemisphere of the brain, while logic is managed in the left hemisphere (theory originated by Roger W. Sperry). When you count, you engage the left, logical side of your brain, and the right, emotional side is turned off. The act of counting also shifts your attention away from your angry thoughts and buys you valuable time to cool down before saying or doing something you'll regret.

3. Breathe with Intention - Consciously breathe very deeply for at least three to four minutes. Be sure to breathe into your diaphragm and not your chest. Place your hand on your stomach as you breathe. If your stomach moves out and back in each time you take a breath, you're doing it correctly. (Your chest shouldn't rise and fall. That's shallow breathing, and it increases anxiety.)

Additional Tip: Count and breathe at the same time: inhale for a count of four (stomach out); exhale for a count of eight (stomach in). This triggers the parasympathetic nervous system, which is responsible for your body's relaxation.

4. Release Tension - Use stress balls to discharge tension. Anger manifests physically, and tension-releasing exercises help your body let go of non-productive energy. They increase relaxation and decrease the likelihood of angry outbursts.

a. Progressive Muscle Relaxation - Relax your muscles using a two-step process. First, purposefully tense a muscle group for a count of five, then release it. For example, hands: make fists and pretend that you're squeezing lemons. Squeeze as hard as you can. Don't leave one drop of juice! Then release. Neck and shoulders: pretend you're a frightened turtle pulling your head into your shell. Squeeze your shoulders up to your ears as high as you can, then release. Stomach: pretend that you're lying on your back and an elephant is about to step on your stomach. Tense your stomach as hard as you can so you don't get squished, then release. As you release the tension, notice how soft and heavy your muscles feel. Repeat the tension/release cycle three times for each muscle group. This exercise lowers your overall stress level.

5. Relaxation Skills - In addition to the breathing and tension-releasing exercises, use visualization and meditation to relax.

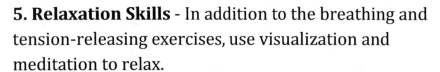

a. Visualization - Imagine yourself in a relaxing environment, such as sitting on the beach as the sun's rays warm you.

b. Meditation - Watch your thoughts come and go without reacting to them. Find a quiet place to sit, or stay where you are if you can't leave, and observe each thought that comes into your head. You can imagine you're reading the thought as it passes by on a revolving digital display, or you can imagine putting the thought into a helium balloon and watching it disappear into the sky. If sitting still is challenging for you, do a walking meditation. Walk around a familiar neighborhood or a track so that you don't have to pay close attention to your route. Meditation is a very grounding exercise, whether you do it for a minute or an hour.

6. Listen to music – Your favorite music can calm and put you in a better mood.

7. Exercise – Physical activity reduces anger. Take out your frustration on your bike or the pavement as you run. Exercising releases endorphins - "happy hormones" - that lift your mood and reduce your pain perception.

NOTE: Hitting punching bags or other objects may be helpful for people who become passive when they're angry. However, this activity increases adrenaline and reinforces aggressive behavior in people who already struggle with physical hostility.

CALL TO ACTION: Choose *one* quick tip that you will commit to trying this week.

Time to Reflect

We've all been there: You lost your cool, and you know it wasn't a good way to deal with a situation. You feel bad, but you think, "There's nothing I can do about it now." Well, yes and no. It's true that you can't go back and change the past. But you can take steps to affect your future by handling the next conflict differently. One essential step toward changing your behavior is to *reflect* (or look back) on what happened during an angry episode. When we reflect on what happened, and what our contribution to the problem was, we condition our brakes to stop bad behavior faster the next time we're in a heated situation. Let's look at some reflection techniques:

1. **Write About It** - Writing is a safe way to express and release uncomfortable emotions.

   a. **Journaling:** There are many styles of journaling. Some people use free-style writing to get all of their thoughts and feelings out of them and onto paper, in no particular order. This style of writing is a good choice when you have extreme emotions that would be destructive to express to a person. A more structured way to journal is to divide the entry into three parts:

   Part 1: In this first section, release your anger or frustration by writing about how you felt and how you behaved. This might seem destructive, but getting your thoughts *down on paper* and *out of you* is actually very healing.

   Part 2: Next, process and reflect. Answer questions like "What does this mean about me?", "What would my friend say about this?", "What did I do or say that made the situation worse?", and "What am I afraid will happen?"

   Part 3: Finally, set goals for next time and make an action plan. How would I like to shift my behavior? How would that benefit my relationship? What is my plan for making this shift? How will I deal with obstacles along the way to changing my habits?

b. **Letter Writing:** Write a letter to someone you're upset with. This is NOT a letter that you will send. (It's best to write on paper or in a Word document and not in an email, since accidentally hitting "Send" could make the situation worse.) Say everything you want to in the letter. You can use sentence starters like, "It really hurt me when....", "I wish that...", and "All I really wanted was...." This can be a cathartic experience.

2. Positive Self-Talk – Review a list of affirmations. When you direct your attention to positive truths, you invite pleasant feelings. Anger creates negative energy in your body. Use positive self-talk to counter it:

a. "I'm in the driver's seat."
b. "I'm learning to deal with my anger."
c. "This is temporary. I'm mad right now, but when I calm down, I'll be able to better understand this situation."

3. Talk to Someone You Trust – Call someone who is safe and supportive. This person is a good listener and offers helpful feedback.

4. Use Humor – Ask yourself, "What's funny about this situation?" Learn to laugh. Find humor in even the darkest moments. Watch a funny movie or TV show.

CALL TO ACTION: This week, choose *one* reflection technique that you can commit to using.

What's My Communication Style?

Have you ever wondered how a conversation can turn ugly really fast? Maybe you say one thing - or don't say one thing - and the next thing you know, you're fighting with someone? It's very easy for this to happen when one or both people do not use an assertive communication style. If your communication style isn't assertive, then it's passive, aggressive, or passive-aggressive, and none of these three styles will get you what you want.

What does it mean to be passive, aggressive, or passive-aggressive? Read the following descriptions, and see which style you tend to use:

Passive – You don't speak up. Even if you're bothered by something, you hold it in. People don't understand you, and you don't get your needs met.

Aggressive – You speak and act in ways that hurt others. Yelling, cursing, name-calling, and getting physical are all examples of aggressive behavior.

Passive – Aggressive – You show how you feel rather than say how you feel. Have you ever had a frown on your face and your arms crossed in front of your chest, but when someone asked you, "What's wrong?" you said, "Nothing"? That's passive-aggression. Sarcasm is another example of passive aggression. Someone shows up late to a study group and you say, "Oh, wow...so nice of you to join us." That's passive-aggressive. We think we are being "nice" by keeping things "light" and not saying what we actually feel. But in the end, the other person can tell you're irritated. When we try to lighten things up with sarcasm, we send mixed signals and complicate matters.

Assertive – You express your thoughts and feelings respectfully, even though people may not like what you have to say: "Next time you're going to be late, I'd like it if you'd give me a call or text me." If you say it in a calm, polite way, you cut down on the chances of getting into a fight.

Although we might use different communication styles at different times, there's usually one we use more often than others.

What's your go-to communication style?

_____

Where did you learn to use this style?

_____

How does this style help you?

_____

How does this style hurt you?

_____

What have others said to you about your style?

_____

CALL TO ACTION: This week, pay attention to how you communicate with others. Perhaps you communicate differently with your family and your friends. Are you passive? Aggressive? Passive-aggressive? Assertive? Expressing your needs in a calm, polite way will improve your interactions with others.

Are You Listening?

We've been talking about how to communicate your thoughts and feelings to others. Now let's talk about something equally important: *listening*. How does someone know you're listening to them? How can you tell if someone is listening to you? When you need to talk to someone about a private problem, do you seek out certain people more than others? Have you ever wondered why? Most likely it's because they are good *active listeners*.

Although it can be helpful to get support from someone outside of a difficult situation, sometimes the only way to resolve it is to speak directly with the person you're upset with. Conversations between people who have ongoing conflict can be tricky, but if you can both show up as good listeners, you have a shot at getting your issue worked out with minimum frustration.

Use the following active listening techniques to turn an important conversation from destructive to productive.

HELPFUL LISTENING HABITS

1. **Encourage the person to talk**: *"You seem upset. Want to talk about it? Sometimes talking helps."*

2. **Allow Silences**: Even if the speaker pauses, don't interrupt. Let them gather their thoughts or get the courage to say something they've been holding back.

3. **Paraphrase/Restate:** Check in with the person to make sure you understand what they mean. "So what you're saying is that it hurt your feelings when I didn't call. Is that right?"

4. **Reflect:** Repeat back some of the emotions the person is trying to express. "It sounds like you're feeling *taken advantage of* by your friend."

5. **Acknowledge and Validate:** Let the other person know you understand what they're feeling: "It makes sense you were upset when I didn't come to your party."

6. **Share and Self-Disclose:** Share similar feelings and experiences you've had. This can comfort the speaker by letting them know they're not alone or "crazy". Be careful not to hijack the conversation. The focus stays on the other person; you're just letting them know you've "been there".

7. **Interpret:** Offer alternative interpretations of what the person is upset about. "Is it possible she didn't see you when you passed each other?"

8. **Point Out Consequences:** If the person is emotionally ready to look at how they may be adding to a problem, help them to see their part. Be kind and gentle – don't put them on the defensive. "When you yell at your parents, do you end up getting what you want?"

9. **Redirect:** If talking is getting the person more angry or worked up, that may be a sign that it's time to change the subject or continue the conversation at a later time.

10. **Sum Up:** Draw the conversation to a close by deciding on a goal and making a plan. "Since you want to raise your algebra grade, what do you think about asking your teacher what you need to do to raise it?"

Try using as many active listening techniques as possible as you respond in the following scenarios.

1. Your mother tells you:
   I'm sick of you being on your phone all day. I just want to have dinner without your phone.
2. Your brother tells you:
   You never help out around the house. I end up having to do your chores to keep you out of trouble with Mom and Dad.
3. Your friend tells you:
   My boyfriend is not calling me, and I've called him so many times. He always does this to me. Why does he hate me so much?

Finally, some tips on what *not* to do when someone is talking to you. What message do you think it sends to the speaker when we're distracted? When we interrupt?

HARMFUL LISTENING HABITS

1. Judging what the speaker is saying. *"That's stupid."*
2. Assuming you know what the speaker is about to say and interrupting.
3. Not keeping your emotions in check about what's being said.
4. Changing the subject without acknowledging that you're doing so.
5. Being distracted while someone is talking to you. *Put your phone away.*
6. Thinking about what you'll say in response instead of really listening.
7. Offering a solution when the person hasn't asked for one.

CALL TO ACTION: Practice active listening skills with those close to you.

Your Body Speaks

What is body language? Why is it important for us to know how we use body language to communicate? What types of things do you do with your body to show that you're angry?

The following is a list of things we do with our bodies that communicate negativity. Place a checkmark next to the ones you do.

Eyes:

- ☐ Glaring
- ☐ Rolling
- ☐ Narrowing focus
- ☐ Refusing to look at the target person

Body:

- ☐ Crossing arms
- ☐ Biting lips
- ☐ Pointing finger at someone or making a shaming gesture
- ☐ Covering ears
- ☐ Clenching fists

Breathing:

- ☐ Breathing hard
- ☐ Holding breath

Making noises:

- ☐ Sighing
- ☐ Lip smacking

If your body could speak, what would it say?

Why do you think you use your body instead of using your words?

CALL TO ACTION: This week, pay attention to your body language when you're upset. Practice using your words instead.

You've Got Me All Wrong!

Since you're reading this book, it's probably safe to say that your communication style is not always assertive. What do you know about your own style so far? Are you finding that it's indirect? Aggressive? Knowing your style is half the battle toward changing it. The next step is working on becoming more assertive. The "Stay Away From" list is a useful tool for this. It's a list of words and phrases known to turn a conversation in a negative direction.

STAY AWAY FROM:

1. Absolute words, like "always" and "never". Absolute words put the listener on the defense because the words are usually not accurate.

   a. Always – "You always do that." Instead say, "I don't like it when you _____ ."
   b. Never – "You never listen."
      Instead say, "I don't feel heard," or "I'd like for you to give me your undivided attention."
   c. Everyone – "Everyone else has an iPhone."
      Instead say, "I'd like an iPhone."
   d. No one – "No one likes me."
      Instead say, "I want to make more friends."

2. Proving that you're right, smarter, etc.

"I told you so." We say this to make sure the other person knows we were right. Although we may *have* been right, throwing it in the other person's face pushes them away, creates defensiveness, and lessens your chances of getting your needs met. (Remember, they *know* you told them so and probably already feel embarrassed! You don't need to rub it in.) Instead say, "I'm sorry that happened."

3. "Should/Shouldn't" statements

"You shouldn't wear that." "Should" or "shouldn't" statements suggest that a person is doing something wrong. It can leave the listener feeling ashamed, defensive, and incompetent. Instead say, "I think this one looks great on you."

4. "I know best" statements

"I do it this way, and I never have a problem." This can sound boastful or controlling to the other person. When we're on the receiving end of someone's bragging, we get the message that we can't find what works best for us. Instead say, "One thing I've tried that has worked is...." It's more helpful.

5. Giving advice

Have you ever given someone advice, only to learn they did the opposite? Giving advice sends the message that we know better for someone than they do. Contrary to popular belief, when friends ask for advice, they are usually just struggling with self-doubt. Rather than telling them what to do, ask them what their options are and what they've been thinking about doing. You'll be most useful to a friend who's discovering what's right for them by being a good listener.

6. "You" statements

When we're frustrated with something someone is doing, it's easy to focus on the behavior we don't like. But when we start a sentence with "You...," for example, "*You* didn't do the dishes," the person will feel attacked and try to defend themselves. Instead, talk about yourself. Use "I" statements to express your own concerns and needs. "I'd like you to do the dishes." "I" statements will be explained further in the next session.

7. Asking "Why" questions

"Why" questions are accusatory. You may think you're asking because you're curious, but when you're angry ask "Why…?", it's usually because you dislike what someone has done. If you're genuinely curious about something, it's okay to ask "Why?" For example, "Why is the sky blue?" But asking "Why did you do that?!" is a loaded question. There's no right answer the person can give you. Instead say, "I don't like it when you do that."

8. Don't bring other people into your conversation.

Saying something like "Your friend says the same thing about you" weakens your position. It sends the message that your own point of view isn't valid in and of itself. Your feelings matter, regardless of whether others feel the same way or not.

CALL TO ACTION: This week, count how many times you do things from the "Stay Away From" list. Don't get discouraged. Remember, awareness is power!

Getting What I Want
The Power of Assertive Communication

Now that you know your communication style and what words and phrases to stay away from, it's time to learn how to get what you want by using assertive communication. Being assertive is expressing your thoughts and feelings in a direct and respectful way. To help with this, use the following format. Once you get used to it, you can play around with the words and make them your own.

(1) I feel _____ (feeling word) (2) when you _____ (specific behavior).
(3) I understand that _____(explain what you understand).
(4) I'd like_____(state what you want).
(5) This is important to me because _____(list reasons).
(6) Some alternatives are _____(state what else would be ok with you).

For example, let's use a situation where you're upset with your parent for going through your social media accounts. Here's how you would use the format to express yourself assertively:

(1) I feel frustrated (2) when you delete my social media accounts during random checks of my phone. (3) I understand that I've posted inappropriate things in the past and that's why you check my phone now. (4) I'd like for you to tell me when you find inappropriate stuff and you're going to delete my account. (5) This is important to me because I want to save my favorite pictures. (6) An alternative could be that I add you as a follower on my accounts so you can see my posts and let me know right away if you have a problem with them.

1. Use "I" statements. Statements that start with "I" are very powerful. For one, they give the listener space to hear what you have to say. When you

talk about yourself and not the other person, you lessen the likelihood that the other person will get defensive. When you start a statement with "You", for example, "You did it wrong," the other person will hear it as an attack. They'll begin forming a counterattack and you won't get what you want. "I" statements are also powerful because they are very hard to argue. If you say that you feel hurt, the other person can't argue that you don't feel hurt.

    a. Format to follow: "I feel _____."

    b. For example: "I feel hurt."

    c. Be sure to use a feeling word (uncomfortable, sad, nervous, etc.) after the word "feel". People often make the mistake of saying, "I feel that you are...." There is no such feeling as "that you are...."

2. State the specific behavior that bothered you (what the person said/did).

    a. Format to follow: "...when you _____...."

    b. For example: "...when you deleted my social media accounts...."

3. Tell the person why you think they did what they did, and let them know what it is that you understand. People like to be understood. This usually reduces the likelihood of defensiveness.

    a. Format to follow: "I understand that_____."

    b. For example: "I understand that you're worried about what I'm doing online, and you want to make sure I'm safe."

4. State your request in one brief sentence. Remember not to use a demanding tone.

    a. Format to follow: "I'd like for you to _____."

    b. For example: "I'd like for you to talk to me before you delete my social media accounts."

5. Say why your request is important to you. It helps to give at least two reasons.

    a. Format to follow: "This is important to me because _____."

    b. For example: "This is important to me because my friends reach out to me through my accounts and I don't want them to think I'm ignoring them. Also, when you delete my accounts I lose my favorite photos."

6. Provide some alternatives to your request so that solving the problem is a collaborative effort. Giving some choices can help the other person feel more motivated to work with you and increases the likelihood of change.
    a. Format to follow: "Some other ways around this could be to _____," or "If you can't _____, then can you _____?"
    b. For example: "Some other ways around this could be to tell me you want to go through my accounts and I'll go through them with you," or "If you can't tell me before you go through my accounts, then can you tell me that you're worried about me and I will be open with you?"

Does this sound like a lot of words to you? Guess how long it should take to express yourself with this format? When done correctly, the whole thing should take about 30 seconds to one minute. Some tips to remember:
1. Make your statement only once.
2. Do not repeat your point.
3. Do not bring up another situation that's bothering you. This will weaken the power of the communication.

If you're taking much more than a minute to express yourself, then you need to prepare more in advance.

Ready? Let's practice.

First, think of a situation that bothers you. Summarize it here:

_____

Second, express your feelings, thoughts, and needs around the situation using the format above. Make sure it's brief.

(1) I feel _____, (2) when you _____.

(3) I understand that _____.

(4) I'd like _____.

(5) This is important to me because_____.

(6) Some other options are _____.

Let's reflect.

1. How would you feel if you were on the receiving end of this message?

2. What could you change that would make it more effective?

CALL TO ACTION: Using the tool above, communicate with someone about something that is bothering you.

Use Your Communication Skills
Role Play

Here are some scenarios for you to use to practice your newly learned communication skill. It's OK if some of these situations don't apply to you. Just imagine that you are in the scenario, and that it bothers you.

1. You saw on Instagram/SnapChat that your friends went out without you.

2. Your friend keeps borrowing money and never pays you back.

3. You notice your classmate cheating off of you during a test.

4. Your mom keeps complaining about what you're doing wrong, but doesn't acknowledge what you do right.

5. Your sister doesn't include you when she has her friends over.

6. Your father says negative things about your mother to you.

7. Your mother drinks too much alcohol.

8. Your friend often cancels on you at the last minute.

9. Your friend's parents are more permissive than yours and you feel left out.

10. Your stepparent acts like a parent and you feel uncomfortable.

11. Your boyfriend seems to flirt with other girls at school.

12. You've called your friend several times, but she hasn't responded. You know that she's OK because you see photos of her on Instagram going out and having a good time.

13. Your parents comment on everything you eat.

14. You share something personal with your friend, and they tell others at school.

CALL TO ACTION: This week, ask someone what they might do in one of these situations. Talk about whether it would be effective or not.

Understanding Boundaries

Have you ever agreed to do something with someone when you really needed time and space to yourself to relax? Is it hard for you to say no, ask for what you need, or set "boundaries"? If you want to feel less angry, you'll need to get good at setting boundaries.

What Is a Boundary?

An easy way to think about a boundary is to imagine the border of a country. This is an invisible line around a piece of land where people speak their own language, follow certain laws, and practice unique traditions. Just as countries have borders, people have invisible boundaries that keep them feeling safe. For example, let's say someone stands too close to you in line at the supermarket and you feel uncomfortable. That feeling tells you that your personal space is being violated. It's essential to set boundaries when others abuse or violate our space, time, body, money or emotional vulnerability. When we protect ourselves, we are less likely to be angry.

Where Do Boundaries Come From?

We learn boundaries from our caregivers: parents, family members, friends, teachers, coaches, etc. We learn boundaries by watching others. If Mom runs herself ragged with her job, housework, volunteering, and never says, "No, I'm sorry. I can't work the school bake sale...," then you learn that it's OK to overwork yourself. We learn boundaries from the way we are treated by others. If Dad yells at you a lot, then you grow up believing that being yelled at is OK, and you accept this behavior from others because you're used to it. There's also a good chance you'll become a yeller and violate others yourself. The good news about the fact that boundaries are learned is that they can be *unlearned*. If you start paying attention to your gut reactions, they will guide you in setting boundaries. You'll learn to say things like, "It's not OK for you to talk to me that way," or "Sorry, but I don't let people copy my homework."

Types of Boundaries

1. Physical Boundaries create enough space between you and another person so that you feel comfortable. Examples:

    a. You keep a certain distance from people when standing in the lunch line at school. If someone is standing too close, you take a step forward.

    b. Your friend wants to leave a pile of her belongings in your bedroom while she travels out of town, and you say no.

2. Emotional Boundaries are invisible buffers that protect us from people who do things that hurt our feelings. Examples:

    a. Your mother complains to you about your father and demands

that you comfort her.
    b. Your boyfriend or girlfriend cheats on you.

3. Intellectual Boundaries include our good ideas and scholarly achievements. Examples:

    a. A student cheats on a test by copying your answers.
    b. A partner takes credit for your ideas in a class project.

4. Sexual Boundaries keep us safe from unwanted touching and inappropriate sex talk. Examples of sexual boundary violations:

    a. Someone touches you inappropriately or manipulates you into doing something sexual that you don't want.
    b. Your uncle tells you a sexually inappropriate joke.

5. Financial Boundaries keep our money from being misused or stolen. Examples:

    a. A friend borrows money from you but doesn't repay it.
    b. You inherit money from a grandparent and your parent takes it.

Problematic Boundaries: Boundaryless or Walled-In

People who are "boundaryless" give too much, trust too easily, and have difficulty saying no. They are taken advantage of and get into harmful relationships. At the other end of the extreme, people can be "walled-in". They mistrust others and keep them at great distances. People with walled-in boundaries feel lonely and isolated. Ideally, we want to avoid being boundaryless and walled-in, and set healthy, moderate boundaries that keep us both safe and connected. (See **Setting Boundaries: Where Do I Draw the Line?**)

Exercise

List some of your boundaries:

1. _____
2. _____
3. _____

Do people know about your boundaries? Do they respect your boundaries? Are there boundaries that you need to loosen or strengthen?

CALL TO ACTION: This week, pay attention to your gut reactions to your surroundings: the things people say, favors they ask, how close to or far from you they stand, how and where they touch you, etc. What does it feel like? Ask yourself, "Do I like that or not?" Your answers will help you to set healthy boundaries.

Where Do You Draw the Line?
Setting Boundaries

When is it OK to say no? How much is too much? Can I ask for more time? Can I ask for more space? When it comes to setting boundaries, people are often unsure of themselves. They don't know what to ask for. They wonder if their requests are reasonable.

When Is It Crucial to Be Aware of Your Boundaries?

1. When you find yourself habitually putting others' needs before your own
2. When you're asked to share more information about yourself than you feel comfortable sharing
3. When you're asked to do something that goes against your values
4. When someone is too close to or touching you in a way you don't like
5. When you simply don't *want* to do something

As discussed in "Understanding Boundaries", one of the keys to keeping calm is setting limits with others. When we loan money to people who don't repay it, or stay on the phone for hours with friends who talk only about themselves and don't ask about us, we're likely to get frustrated. Healthy boundaries are set according to what feels comfortable, and that will vary from person to person. Knowing yourself well is crucial. Once you identify what feels good and what feels bad, you can set limits and assertively communicate your desires to others.

Let's look at some strategies for setting healthy boundaries.

Helpful Tips for Setting Limits

1. Be confident. You have the right to say no and you aren't doing anything wrong when you say it. "I'm sorry, but that won't work for me right now" is a reasonable response to a request. No one can argue that it *will* work for you.

Be prepared for the person to be upset. It's OK for them to have their feelings about it.

2. It's OK to say, "I have other plans." Even staying home and watching TV is a plan.

3. Don't beat yourself up for saying no. Remind yourself that your feelings matter just as much as others'.

4. Ask for time to make your decision: "I can let you know my answer tomorrow (next week, etc.)."

5. Feel free to offer alternatives to the request: "I'm not available to work the fundraiser all day, but I can work from 9-12 PM, if that would help," or "I'm not comfortable giving you my homework to copy, but I'm happy to help you with the assignment after school."

How Can I Set Limits Around Requests?

1. Repeat back to the person what you understand they're asking for. If you're uncertain, ask for clarification.
2. Evaluate whether or not the request is something you want to do.
3. Tell the person whether or not you'll be able to do it. Be honest and say yes or no. You don't need to come up with excuses.
   For example: "I get that you want to borrow some money. You haven't paid me back for the concert tickets, so I don't feel comfortable lending you more right now." Some people worry that if they set a boundary like

this, the friendship will end. If that's the case, think about the value of a "friendship" that only exists if you do things you don't want to. It can help to ask others (with healthy boundaries) what they would do in your situation. Ask *yourself*, "Would I end a friendship if my friend didn't loan me money?"

Exercise 1: Practice Setting a Boundary with Requests

Think about a request you'd feel uncomfortable doing. Write it below:

Request: _____

Now practice setting a boundary. What do you say?

Response to Request: _____

What If I'm Uncomfortable in the Moment?

Say that you feel uncomfortable. Ask the person to stop, move, etc.

For example: I feel uncomfortable when you _____ (specific behavior). Please stop _____.

Exercise 2: Practice Setting a Boundary When You're Uncomfortable in the Moment

Think about a situation that makes you feel uncomfortable (for example, someone standing too close). Write it below:

Situation: _____

Now practice setting a boundary. What do you say or do? (Your response might be an action instead of words.)

Response to Situation:

_____

_____

Remember: Setting a boundary can be as easy as saying "I'd like for you to _____ , " or "I don't like when you _____ ."

Some contents adapted from Matthew McKay, PhD and Peter Rogers

CALL TO ACTION: This week practice setting boundaries.

What's Your Pattern?

Unhealthy Belief	Hurtful Thought	Feelings	Destructive Behavior	Consequence
I have to win arguments, otherwise I'm a loser.	If I don't win this argument, he'll think he's better than me.	Anxious, angry, and fearful.	I don't listen to his point of view, but keep interrupting him.	He ends the friendship. I feel embarrassed because I know this is my issue.
Healthy Belief	Helpful Thought	Feelings	Constructive Behavior	Consequence
In healthy arguments people take turns speaking and listening. It's not about winning or losing.	I feel good about myself when I communicate in a healthy way, even when it's hard.	Confident and connected to my friend.	I continue to listen to the points he makes, and he listens to mine. We are able to disagree respectfully.	We continue to value our friendship.
Unhealthy Belief	Hurtful Thought	Feelings	Destructive Behavior	Consequence
My parents don't understand me.	They don't let me do anything because they have no idea what it's like to be a teen.	Misunderstood, angry, hurt, and alone.	I scream at my parents, "Leave me alone!", go to my room, and slam my door.	My parents are confused and upset about my reaction and take away my phone.
Healthy Belief	Helpful Thought	Feelings	Constructive Behavior	Consequence
I may not like what my parents say, but I know they have my best interests at heart.	I wish they would let me go see my friends, but I know I need to finish my homework.	Loved, and a little left out because I'm not with my friends.	I stay home and study instead of seeing my friends.	I get better grades and see my friends on the weekend.

Exercise: Fill in the remaining boxes in the first two rows, come up with your own unhealthy and healthy beliefs.

Unhealthy Belief	Hurtful Thought	Feelings	Destructive Behavior	Consequence
I can't seem weak.				
Healthy Belief	**Helpful** Thought	Feelings	**Constructive** Behavior	Consequence
It's okay to be myself.				
Unhealthy Belief	**Hurtful** Thought	Feelings	**Destructive** Behavior	Consequence
Healthy Belief	**Helpful** Thought	Feelings	**Constructive** Behavior	Consequence

Stop! Reframe Your Thinking

When you feel upset, do you ask yourself why? Would you believe that you feel upset when you think upsetting thoughts? Our thoughts directly impact our emotions. Do you pay attention to your thoughts? If your thoughts are negative and irrational, then most likely you'll feel upset. Reframing your thoughts will increase your positive emotions. The purpose of this exercise is to help you perceive situations in a more neutral, realistic way so that you can feel better.

Angry Thoughts	Reframing Thoughts
He did that on purpose. I'll show him.	1. How do I know he did that intentionally? Perhaps he didn't realize that it was going to affect me. 2. Even if I show him, he may have no idea what lesson I'm trying to teach him.
She should have understood that.	1. Though I would like for everyone to be on the same page, it's not always possible. 2. Just because I understand doesn't mean everyone else does.
She took advantage of me.	1. She can only take advantage of me if I let her. I need to set better boundaries. 2. She just asks for favors, and I have the right to say "No".
He caused me to be angry.	1. No one caused me to be angry. I am angry because of how I view the event. 2. It sounds like I want to blame my emotions on someone else, when I know it has to do with my own expectation.

Exercise: Let's put this into practice.

Instructions: List your own angry thoughts in the first column, and try to reframe your thoughts in the second column (at least two reframing thoughts per angry thought).

Angry Thoughts	Reframing Thoughts

CALL TO ACTION: Reframe your upsetting thoughts daily. If you practice this skill consistently, you'll notice positive changes in your thoughts and feelings. And guess what? You won't need to do much work with this later because reframing will become natural and automatic to you.

Looking at It Differently
Using Rational Emotive Therapy

Imagine two students get a B on an exam. One student is happy about the grade; the other is very upset. If both students get the same grade on the same test, why do they feel so differently? The answer is that *our emotions come from our THOUGHTS about a situation, and not from the situation itself.*

If student 1 gets a B and thinks, "This is a good grade - definitely above average. I wonder if I could get an A next time," he will feel calm, because he's having a reasonable thought. If student 2 gets a B and thinks, "I'm a loser," she'll feel upset, because she's having an upsetting thought. This thought comes from her painful belief that her self-worth goes up and down with her grades.

Why would two people have such different thoughts about the same event? Our thoughts are determined by our core beliefs about ourselves, the world, and our future. Student 1 has the core belief, "I do my best and then challenge myself to do better." Student 2 has the core belief, "I'm only valuable when I make straight A's." We feel the way we think. If we view a situation in a negative light, we feel negative emotions. If we view it in a positive, or at least neutral light, we feel better.

Rational Emotive Therapy (R.E.T.) is a tool that can improve our perception of ourselves, others, and life in general. If you want to feel better, the first step is becoming aware of your triggering thoughts and then writing them down.

Exercise: Over the next few days, when you feel angry, describe the **situation** you're in. Next, write your **interpretation** (the thought you had) about it. Then, try to pinpoint the **feelings** that came up for you, as well as the **actions**

you took. Finally, if your own thinking triggered you to feel angry, **dispute (argue)** your interpretation and choose alternative thoughts. Below is an example of what R.E.T. looks like:

1. ***Situation:*** What was the situation that led you to become angry?
2. ***Belief:*** What is the belief you hold in general about this subject?
3. ***Interpretation (thought):*** How did you interpret the situation?
4. ***Feelings:*** What were your feelings during the situation?
5. ***Actions:*** If you felt anger, what did you do because of your anger?
6. ***Dispute/Argue:*** How can you look at the situation differently?

You can alter your thoughts and feelings by changing your beliefs. How does this work? Beliefs shape the way we think, and our thoughts create our feelings. When we feel a certain way, we act a certain way. The following diagram shows how this idea flows:

Beliefs ⟹ **Thoughts** ⟹ **Feelings** ⟹ **Actions**

For the final step of the R.E.T. process, we argue or "dispute" our original belief until we have more helpful ways of looking at the situation. Use the following questions to help you argue your belief:

➤ Who said that this is true? Where is the evidence?
➤ Why do I believe this?
➤ What are some alternative ways of looking at this?

The following is an example of how to use R.E.T. for anger:

Situation: I shared something personal with a friend, and he told others.

Belief: Friends should keep secrets, otherwise they're not good friends.

Interpretation (thought): He's not a good friend.

Feelings: Betrayed and angry.

Actions: I yelled at him for not keeping his mouth shut.

Dispute: As I think about the situation, I remember that I, too, have shared my friend's personal information with others. And I didn't do it to hurt him. I guess it's not that easy to hold a secret.

Try out R.E.T. with a situation from your own life:

Situation: _____

Belief: _____

Interpretation: _____

Feelings: _____

Action: _____

Dispute: _____

CALL TO ACTION: This week, identify one of your core negative beliefs about yourself, the world, or your future.

Bullying

Most people have heard about bullying, witnessed bullying, been the victim of a bully, or have been a bully themselves. Statistics on bullying are pretty bleak: every seven minutes a child is bullied; adults intervene in bullying 4% of the time; peers intervene 11% of the time; and 85% of the time there is no intervention at all.

What is Bullying?

Bullying is being "habitually cruel, insulting, or threatening to others who are weaker, smaller, or in some way vulnerable." (www.merriam-webster.com)

Bullying can be:

- Physical – punching, kicking, biting, pushing, pulling hair, stealing, etc.
- Emotional – name-calling, teasing, threatening, gossiping
- Sexual – humiliating someone verbally about gender or sexuality, touching someone's body inappropriately, posting inappropriate photos online
- Cyber-bullying – posting photos, stories, or videos on social media (online or via text) that are hurtful to others.

According to a study conducted in 2010 by Nixon and Davis, 55% of students report being bullied because of their looks; 37% say they're targeted because of their body shape; and 16% say they're bullied because of their race. Students with disabilities are bullied two to three times more than their peers (Marshall, Kendall, Banks & Gover (Eds.), 2009), and 82% of LGBTQ students said they were bullied in the last year for their sexual orientation (National School Climate Survey, 2011). www.pacerkidsagainstbullying.org/wp-content/uploads/2014/07/bullying101tab.pdf

Who Bullies?

Anyone can be a bully. No matter their size, gender, age, grade, race, or ethnicity.

Why Do People Bully?

If parents or other kids have bullied us, we often end up bullying others. We do it as a way of trying to get our power back. Sometimes we think bullying will help us fit in. Maybe we hope that if we bully others, no one will notice our imperfections.

Break the Bullying Cycle

Some bullies argue that no one cares about their bullying – that it's "not that bad". But there are many people in your life who care, such as parents, siblings, friends, teachers, and classmates. Most importantly, though, the person who is being bullied cares...a lot. (See **Put Yourself in My Shoes**.)

When we bully others, it shows a lack of respect. If we lack respect for others, there's a good chance that we don't respect ourselves. Where do you think this lack of respect comes from? Do we learn it at home? From our peers? How can you learn to respect yourself? *How can you respect yourself when you're hurting others?* Maybe you hurt others in an effort to get your pain or anger out. But your pain and anger will stay with you until you talk about your experience with someone you trust. It can help you feel a lot better, and it will strengthen your friendships and other relationships as well.

Do You Feel Good After You Bully Someone?

Are you jealous of your peers? Afraid you're not as smart or popular as someone else in school? You're not the only person who feels this way. There are many others who share your fears, yet find helpful ways of managing their emotions and behavior. Be curious about what they do to feel better when they're struggling with low self-esteem. What do they do instead of bullying?

Effects of Bullying

Bullying can have very serious consequences for victims: depression, anxiety, self-harm (like cutting or burning), problems sleeping or eating, decrease in school participation, falling grades, and suicide. Teens who bully are more likely to:

- abuse alcohol and other drugs
- get into physical altercations
- vandalize property
- drop out of school
- engage in sexual activity at a young age
- get traffic violations
- be convicted of crimes
- go to jail
- abuse partners/children

(https://www.stopbullying.gov/at-risk/effects/#bullied)

Exercise:

Think about a time when you bullied someone:

What did you do?_____

Who was the victim?_____

What do you regret about it? (Why was it bad?) _____

_____

What were you trying to accomplish?_____

_____

How could you accomplish the same thing without hurting anyone?_____

_____

CALL TO ACTION: Talk to a trusted adult (parent, teacher, counselor, etc.) about how to stop the cycle of bullying. (www.stompoutbullying.org)

Fat... Stupid... Ugly

We all know what it's like to be called a name. We've all probably called someone a name. Either way, it feels pretty bad and doesn't help us get what we want. Name-calling makes people shut down and cut off from us. It's a sign that we feel powerless and forced to resort to a low form of communication.

That doesn't mean, however, that judging people is all bad. In fact, making judgements about others is sometimes necessary to stay safe. Let's take a look at the advantages and disadvantages of labeling and making judgements about people.

Advantages of Being Judgmental

We need to make judgements about people to decide how much we're going to trust them. For example, if someone has a habit of promising to meet you and then canceling, it's a good idea to judge this person as "unreliable". This judgement keeps us from expecting something from someone who isn't going to give it, and then getting hurt as a result. Making a judgment about someone can even save your life: if someone has a habit of driving drunk, you're wise to decide that it's dangerous to ride with him/her.

Life is full of situations in which you're going to be judged, and for good reason. Colleges boost their reputations by having successful students in attendance. It's in their best interest to accept new applicants with good high school grades - the best indicator of the grades they'll earn in college. Similarly, if you're trying out for a sports team, you're going to be judged on your athleticism. It's in the best interest of the team to choose the best athletes in order to guarantee the most wins.

Disadvantages of Being Judgmental

When we negatively label people out of anger, they feel our judgement and put up emotional walls. They get busy defending themselves and have zero interest in what's upsetting us. Let's say, for example, you share a room with someone who leaves trash and clothes around. If you call them a "pig", they'll probably get defensive and attack back. At the very least, they're not going to feel motivated to clean up the room. But if you can *describe what it is that they are doing that is not OK with you*, you have a much better shot at getting them to change their behavior.

Though it might seem obvious, it's important to note that while we're judging and labeling people, we're engaged in negative thinking. Negative thoughts lead to negative feelings, and negative feelings often lead to behaviors we regret. Even if you don't act on your negative thoughts and feelings, people can sense your hostility. They keep their distance, and deprive you of close relationships.

Where Did I Learn to Judge, Label, and Name-Call?

Maybe you've heard your parents make nasty comments about people. If the waiter at a busy restaurant gets your order wrong and your dad calls him "stupid", you learn to do the same. Bullies get power by intimidating and verbally assaulting others. Maybe you learn that labeling people is a way to empower yourself. You can pick up these habits from friends, siblings, and even television.

When we judge, label and name-call, we're trying to appear superior. We mistakenly think that a good way to feel better about ourselves is to put others down. What are some things you feel insecure about? Do you cave in to peer pressure and treat others badly as a way to fit in with certain groups?

The good news is that judging and labeling others is a learned habit, which means it can be unlearned. It's never too late to unlearn something. The first step is getting honest with yourself about your own bad habits. Do you use any of the following words to describe people?

Stupid • Ugly • Fat • Pig • Nerd • Gay • Slut • Psycho

What's really going on with you when you resort to name-calling. Is there something about the person you see in yourself that you don't like? Are you name-calling instead of doing the harder work of expressing what you don't like about their behavior? Are you calling someone a "psycho" instead of asking them not to call you so often?

Exercise:

1. Name a time when you were judgmental of someone or called them a name.

_____

2. Why do you think you were judgmental?

_____

3. Describe the specific behavior you didn't like.

_____

4. Name a time someone was judgmental of you or called you a name.

_____

5. What was that like?

_____

6. What would you have wanted them to know about you?

_____

CALL TO ACTION: Pay attention to your judgmental thoughts. What it is about the other person's behavior you don't like? How can you say it? For example, if your girlfriend goes out with someone else and you call her a "slut", she'll get defensive and argue. But if you say, "It's not OK with me for you to go out with other people," she can't argue that it *is* OK with you.

Put Yourself in My Shoes
Developing Empathy

Have you ever heard someone say, "Put yourself in my shoes"? What are they asking of you? They want you to see things their way. They're asking for *empathy*.

What Is Empathy?

Empathy is the ability to see someone else's perspective. It's the ability to relate to another person's experience. (*"I've been there…I know what that's like…."*) Empathy is recognizing familiar emotions in another person and letting him/her know that you do. (*"It makes sense that you feel that way…."*) Most importantly, empathy is the emotional and intellectual understanding of another person's thoughts, feelings, and experiences. We get this by remembering times we were in similar situations and had the same thoughts and feelings.

Why Do We Use Empathy?

We empathize with others so we can understand them better. When people sense that we're trying to understand them, trust, openness, and emotional safety build. People are naturally drawn to those they trust. This is true whether we're at home or school. The more you use empathy, the more you'll notice that people appreciate you. Finally, the better your understanding of others' feelings, the less angry you'll feel.

How Do We Use Empathy?

The next time you're in a situation with someone who's upset, see if you can identify what he/she is feeling. If you're unsure, float back over your life to memories of similar scenarios. How did you feel? Hurt? Scared? Frustrated? Let the person know what you remember by expressing it in a kind way. You can say things like, "I know what that feels like. It's awful. You must have felt terrible! I'm so glad you told me." When you do this, you communicate that the person's feelings make sense and you accept them. This is called *validating*. Learning to use empathy is a process that takes time. It can be challenging if the people in your family don't empathize with one another. But making the effort to develop empathy for others will pay off in multiple ways: by reducing conflict, lessening your anger, and strengthening relationships with friends, boy/girlfriends, and family members.

Let's Put Empathy To Work...

Read the following situations. Instead of assuming the worst about why the person is behaving this way, try to imagine more moderate, helpful reasons by putting yourself in his/her shoes. For example, two of your best friends go out and don't invite you. Instead of assuming they're angry at you, acknowledge that you've done the same in the past and it's okay for them to hang out without you.

1. *Situation: Your friend teases you in front of others.*

   _____

2. *Situation: Your parent doesn't allow you to go to a midnight movie on a school night.*

   _____

3. *Situation: Your teacher corrects you in front of your classmates.*

   _____

4. *Situation: You tell a friend a secret, and she shares it with another friend.*

   _____

5. *Situation: While you're having a serious talk with your friend, his phone rings. He interrupts the conversation and takes the call.*

   _____

Empathy and anger are inversely proportional: the more empathy you have, the less angry you'll feel.

CALL TO ACTION: As you go through your week, try to guess how people around you are feeling. Use their facial expressions and body language to help.

The Other Kind of Smart
Understanding Emotional Intelligence

Did you know that there are different kinds of intelligence? "Book smarts" refers to academic education. "Street smarts" is knowing how to stay safe in your city or neighborhood, and IQ (intelligence quotient) measures your reasoning and problem-solving skills. But when dealing with anger, none of these are as important as understanding *feelings*. This kind of know-how is called emotional intelligence, or EI. EI measures how well you recognize, understand and manage emotions. When someone gives you a hug, do you know how that feels for you? When you yell at someone, are you aware of how that affects them? Emotional intelligence is knowing how others' words and actions affect you, how your words and actions affect others, and using that information to develop better relationships.

One of the essential ingredients of emotional intelligence is self-awareness. Self-awareness means knowing what you're thinking and feeling. For some, identifying thoughts and feelings doesn't come easily. If your caregivers don't ask you what you think or how you feel, you've probably learned that your thoughts and feelings don't matter. You've become an expert at ignoring them. If you're ignoring your thoughts and feelings, you're probably not trying to get your needs met. And if you're not getting what you need, you're going to be feeling pretty angry. Make sense? Getting control of your anger starts with knowing what you're thinking and feeling. Once you get to know yourself, this awareness guides you to manage your impulses when you're in uncomfortable situations.

Have you ever experienced any of the following?
- meeting a parent's new boyfriend/girlfriend
- being pressured by friends to drink or do drugs
- someone cheating off you in school
- someone gossiping about you behind your back

- not being invited to a party
- a sad friend turning to you for comfort

How did you behave in that situation? Are you aware of how your words and actions affected the people around you? We can easily hurt others without intending to. Let's say, for example, you want to understand something your friend did. You ask her, "Why did you do that?" Your intention is to understand the situation better, but your friend takes offense because of your tone and use of the word "why", which can be accusatory.

The foundation of anger management is knowing how you and others are feeling. Imagine the power that comes from knowing how you're impacting those around you, and using that information to improve your relationships. When you raise your emotional intelligence, you strengthen connections to friends, family, and, later in life, to those in the business world.

How Others Impact You and You Impact Others

The following exercise will help you to become emotionally smarter.

Exercise: Think of a time your feelings were hurt. Summarize the situation:

_____

_____

_____

1. Did you express your feeling(s)? Yes   No

2. Did the person who hurt you know that they did? Yes   No   I don't know.

3. If yes, what let them know that they hurt you?

_____

Now turn the table...

Think of a time you said or did something that hurt someone else.

1. How do you know it hurt them?

_____

2. Were you aware right away that they were hurt?   Yes   No

3. If yes, what let you know that they were hurt?

_____

CALL TO ACTION: Becoming self-aware is the first step toward improving your emotional intelligence. This week, challenge yourself to get to know yourself better. You'll shift from someone who acts impulsively and regrets it, to someone who is stable and maintains good relationships over time.

Anger is Like...

Read the following anger analogies. What are the top three you relate to the most?

Can of Soda - Anger is like a can of soda. If you shake it and then pop the top immediately, it will explode and spill everywhere. But if you shake it, tap the top a few times, let some time pass, and open the can slowly, the soda won't spew out. (Natalie Zangan).

Brewer - What happens when you leave a coffee maker on for hours after the coffee has finished brewing? The coffee gets too bitter to drink, no matter how much cream and sugar you add to it. Similarly, when a person holds onto their anger and doesn't express it in a healthy way, it continues to "brew". The person becomes so bitter that she loses the ability to express herself in a way that might be helpful or constructive.
Swami, O. Two Types of Anger. Retrieved from http://omswami.com/2012/09/two-types-of-anger.html

Balloon - Anger is like holding air in an untied balloon. If you let the balloon go, it will blast out of your hands and fly crazily around the room. But if you release the opening slowly, you can control the movement of the balloon. To keep control over the way your anger is expressed, you'll have to let the emotion out in a slow and measured way.
Wiley, T. *Anger Management Balloon Analogy.* Retrieved from http://www.adapt-fl.com

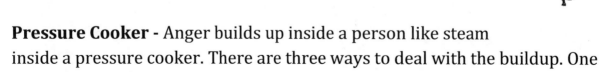

Pressure Cooker - Anger builds up inside a person like steam inside a pressure cooker. There are three ways to deal with the buildup. One way is to keep the pressure inside the cooker until it explodes. Second, you can reduce the pressure by periodically tapping off some of the steam. (This is where the common expressions "venting" and "blowing off steam" come from.) The third (and best) way is to lower the flame and reduce the heat! Rather than stuff anger inside or explode outwardly, express your feeling in a calm and collected way. Stuffing anger harms the self. Exploding anger harms others. Assertive anger - polite, clear and direct - can bring people closer together and help them to get their needs met.

Bushman, B. J. (2013). *Anger Management: What Works and What Doesn't.* Retrieved from https://www.psychologytoday.com/blog/get-psyched/201309/anger-management-what-works-and-what-doesnt

Thunderstorm - Anger is like a thunderstorm with strong winds of crisis and chaos. In the midst of an anger storm, everything is heavy with rain, we can't see anything clearly, and roadways are treacherous. Doop, J. (2012). *A Storm of Anger.* Retrieved from http://realintent.org/a-storm-of-anger/

Iceberg - Anger is like the tip of an iceberg. The part of an iceberg that sticks up above the water is only 10% of the whole thing. Most of it, the other 90%, is under water and hidden from view. When we are experiencing anger and we yell, clench our fists, and slam doors, that's only the "tip" of what's going on with us emotionally. Underneath the anger, and what others can't see, is the largest part of the iceberg: fear, insecurity, frustration, hurt pride, and feelings of disrespect.

Black, B. (2009). *Anger is Like an Iceberg.* Retrieved from https://www.mentalhelp.net/blogs/anger-is-like-an-iceberg/

Poison - Anger is like poison. Once it's in your system, if you want to survive, you'll have to take serious measures to drain it. If you don't, it will eat away at the healthy parts of you until you no longer have control over it.

Rittman, D. (2015). *Lessons Learned from the Bunny Teacher.* Retrieved from http://bunnyteacher.blogspot.com/2015/02/ anger-is-poison-you-must-purge-it-from.html

Create your own anger analogy. How would you describe your anger?

_____

_____

_____

_____

_____

CALL TO ACTION: This week, ask someone which of these analogies they can relate to the most.

Anger Proverbs

The following are proverbs about anger. Which ones can you relate to?

1. The greatest remedy for anger is delay. - unknown

2. If a small thing has the power to make you angry, does that not indicate something about your size? - Syndey J. Harris

3. Where there is anger, there is always pain underneath. - Eckhart Tolle

4. Speak when you are angry and you will make the best speech you will ever regret. - Ambrose Bierce

5. Holding on to anger is like grasping a hot coal with the intent of throwing it at someone else; you are the one who gets burned. - Buddha

6. Never respond to an angry person with a fiery comeback, even if he deserves it…Don't allow his anger to become your anger. -Bohdi Sanders

7. Anger is one letter short of danger. - Eleanor Roosevelt (1884-1962)

8. For every minute you remain angry, you give up sixty seconds of peace of mind. - Ralph Waldo Emerson

9. People won't have time for you if you are always angry or complaining. - Stephen Hawking

10. Whatever is begun in anger ends in shame. - Benjamin Franklin

CALL TO ACTION: Write your own proverb about anger and bring it in next week to share.

Resources

Books

Burns, D., M.D. (1990; 1999). *The Feeling Good Handbook*. The Penguin Group.

Cohen-Posey, K. (2000), *Brief Therapy Client Handouts.* Wiley Publishers.

Davis, M., Ph.D., Paleg, K., Ph.D. & Fanning, P. (2004). *The Messages Workbook*. New Harbinger Publications.

Eifert, G. H., Forsyth, J.P., Hayes, S.C., & McKay, M. (2006), *ACT on Life Not on Anger: The New Acceptance & Commitment Therapy Guide to Problem Anger.* New Harbinger Publications.

Greenberger , D., & Padesky, C. (1995). *Mind Over Mood: Change How You Feel by Changing the Way You Think*. The Guildford Press.

Johnson, S. L. (1997; 2004), *The Therapist's Guide to Clinical Intervention: The 123's of Treatment Planning.* Academic Press, San Diego.

Mellody, P., & Freundlich, L.S., (2003). *The Intimacy Factor: The Ground Rules for Overcoming the Obstacles to Truth, Respect, and Lasting Love.* HarperSanFrancisco.

Potter, R.T., MSW, PhD. (2005), *Handbook of Anger Management: Individual, Couple, Family, and Group Approaches*. The Haworth Clinical Practice Press; The Haworth Reference Press; and imprints of The Haworth Press, Inc.

Schiraldi, G. R., Ph.D., & Kerr, M.H., Ph.D. (2002). *The Anger Management Sourcebook*. McGraw Hill.

Journal Articles

Ellis, A. (1991). The revised ABC's of rational-emotive therapy (RET), *Journal of Rational-Emotive and Cognitive-Behavior Therapy*, Volume 9, Number 3, Page 139.

Pickering, M., Communication in explorations, *A Journal of Research of the University of Maine,* Vol. 3, No. 1, Fall 1986, pp 16-19.

Smith, P. N., & Ziegler, D. J. (2004) Anger and the ABC model underlying Rational-Emotive Therapy, *Psychological Reports*, Vol. 94, pp. 1009-1014.

Blogs and Online Resources

Active Listening Skills. AGING I&R/A TIPS. *Tip Sheet 1.* National Aging Information & Referral Support Center.
http://www.nasuad.org/documentation/I_R/ActiveListening.pdf

Mills, H., Ph.D., *Physiology of Anger.*
http://www.mhcinc.org/poc/view_doc.php?type=doc&id=5805&cn=116

Osho. *Ego - The False Center.* Beyond the Frontier of the Mind.
http://deoxy.org/egofalse.htm

Websites

http://www.stopbullying.gov/at-risk/effects/#bullied

http://www.pacerkidsagainstbullying.org/wp-content/uploads/2014/07/bullying101tab.pdf

http://www.merriam-webster.com

About the Authors

Anita Avedian is a Licensed Marriage and Family Therapist practicing in Tarzana, Sherman Oaks, Hollywood, and Glendale, CA. She graduated with her M.S. in Educational Psychology and certifications in Employee Assistance Program and Human Resources from California State University of Northridge. Her specialties include working with relationships, anger, anxiety, and addictions. Anita Avedian is the Director of Anger Management 818, with nine locations, serving both self-referred and court-ordered individuals seeking help with their aggression.

Anita is the author of the original *Anger Management Essentials* workbook. With over 50 lesson plans, this book has been translated into Spanish, Hebrew, and Armenian. It is used in the Anger Management Essentials certification training, approved by the National Anger Management Association (NAMA). Ms. Avedian is a Certified Anger Management Specialist IV, a Diplomat Member of NAMA, an Authorized NAMA Trainer, and an Anger Management Supervisor, certifying anger management specialists.

Ms. Avedian is also very involved in the professional community. She is the founder of Toastmasters for Mental Health Professionals and cofounder of the California Association of Anger Management Providers, currently the California chapter of NAMA.

Ingrid Caswell is a Certified Anger Management Specialist III and a Marriage and Family Therapist in Beverly Hills, CA. She holds an M.A. in clinical psychology from Antioch University Los Angeles. Her focus of treatment in private practice is trauma and codependency recovery for adults, children, couples, and families. Ms. Caswell facilitates anger management groups and works one-on-one as an executive anger management coach for voluntary and court-ordered clients. She is a member of the National Anger Management Association and serves on the board of the California Association of Anger Management Providers. Ms. Caswell is the co-author and editor of the original *Anger Management Essentials* workbook - the cornerstone resource used in the Anger Management Essentials certification training. She is also one of the founding members of Toastmasters for Mental Health Professionals, where she practices her passion for public speaking.

Made in the USA
San Bernardino, CA
27 November 2018